Waltz Op. 18 in E♭ Major

'Grande Valse Brilliante'

Vivace

BEGINNING CHOPIN FOR PIANO

Boston Music Company

Published by
Boston Music Company

Exclusive Distributors:
Hal Leonard
7777 West Bluemound Road, Milwaukee, WI 53213
Email: info@halleonard.com

Hal Leonard Europe Limited
42 Wigmore Street Maryleborne, London, WIU 2 RY
Email: info@halleonardeurope.com

Hal Leonard Australia Pty. Ltd.
4 Lentara Court Cheltenham, Victoria, 9132 Australia
Email: info@halleonard.com.au

Order No. BM12287
ISBN 1-84609-743-6

This book C Copyright 2006
Boston Music Company

Series Editor David Harrison.
Music edited by Rachel Payne.
Cover designed by Michael Bell Design.
Cover picture courtesy of 'SIPA' Press / Rex Features.

Printed in EU.

www.halleonard.com

Prelude Op. 28, No. 7

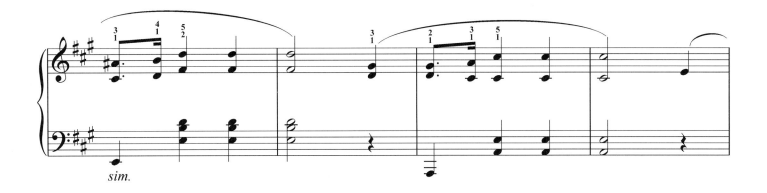

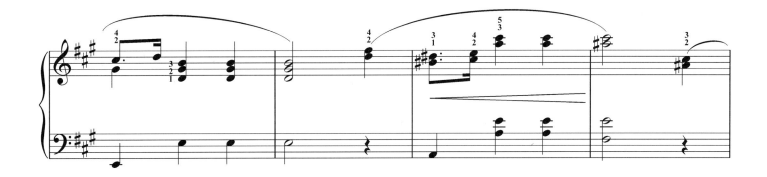

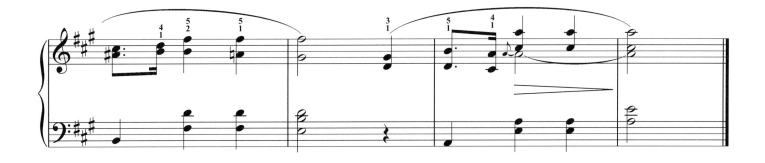

Waltz Op. 69, No. 1

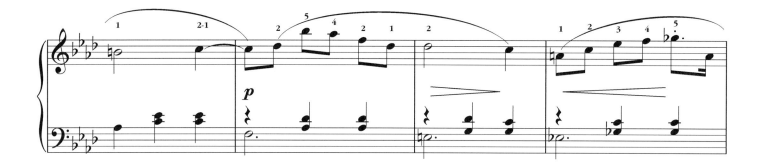

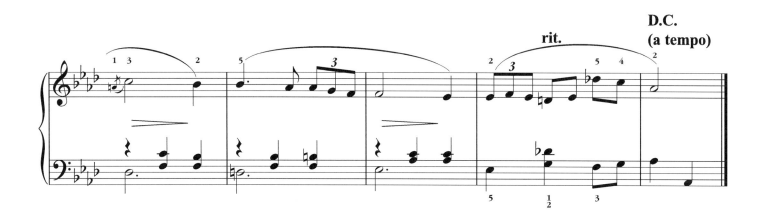

Nocturne Op. 9, No. 2

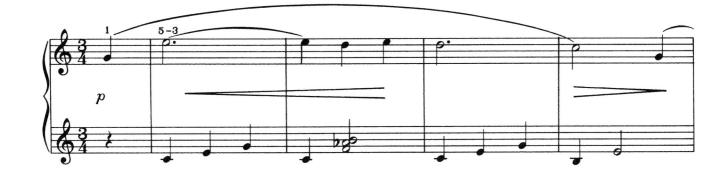

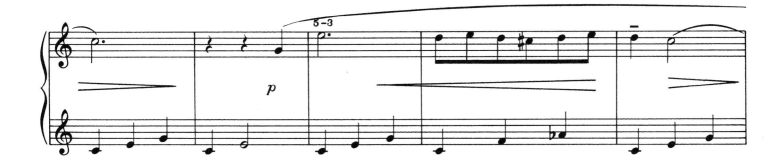

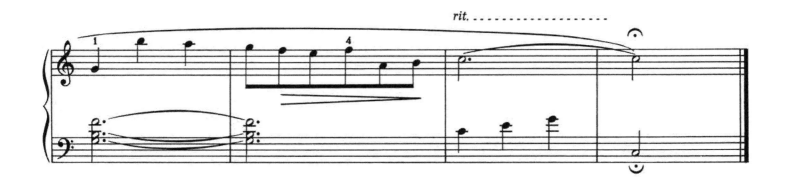

Waltz Op. 70, No. 2

Tempo giusto

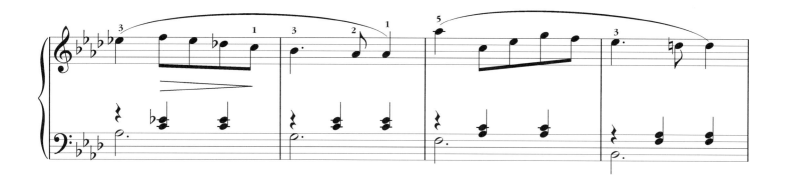

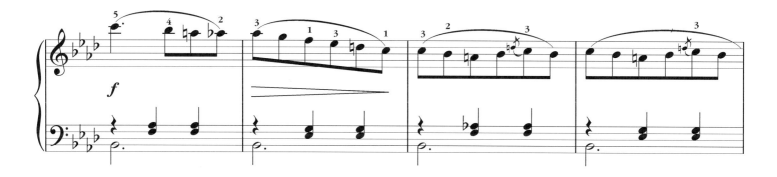

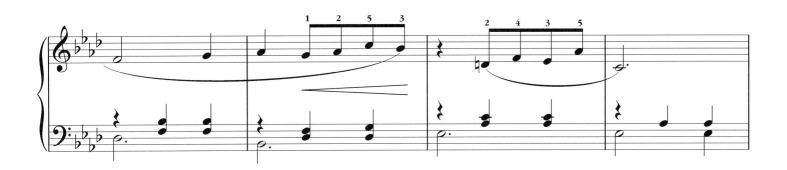

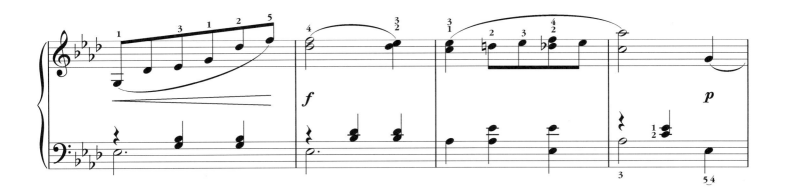

Polonaise Op. 40, No. 1

'Military Polonaise'

Allegro con brio

'Fantaisie' Impromptu Op. 66, No. 4

(Theme)

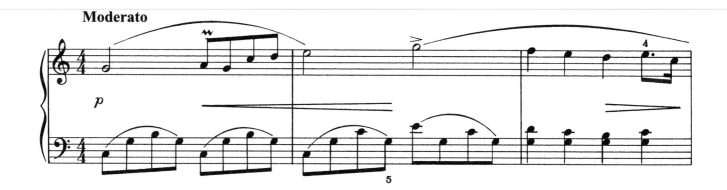

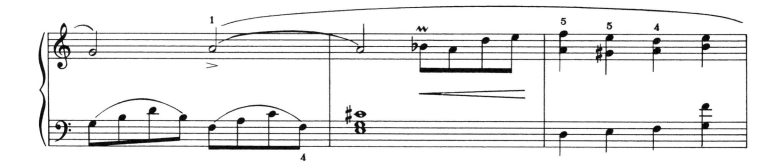

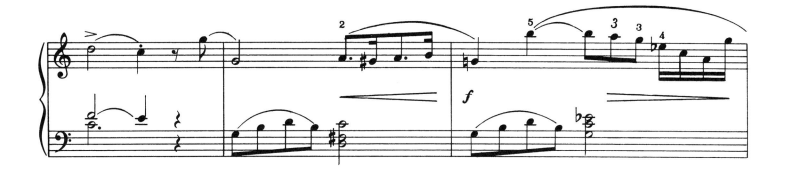

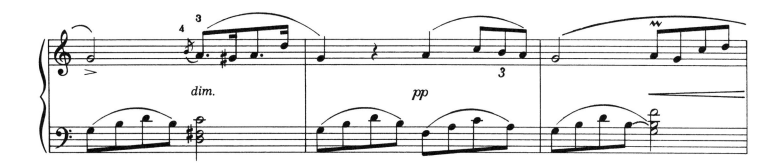

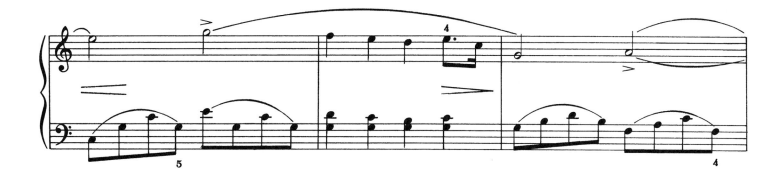

Trio

from Sonata Op. 35, No. 2 ('Funeral March')

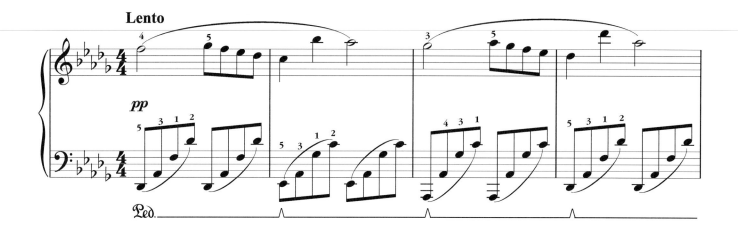

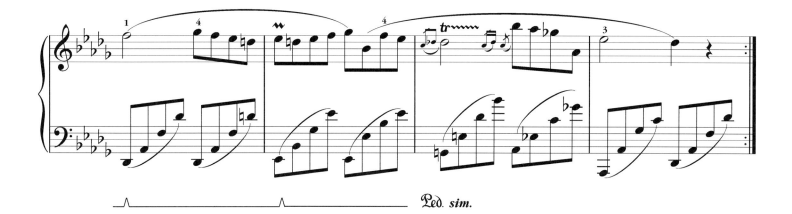

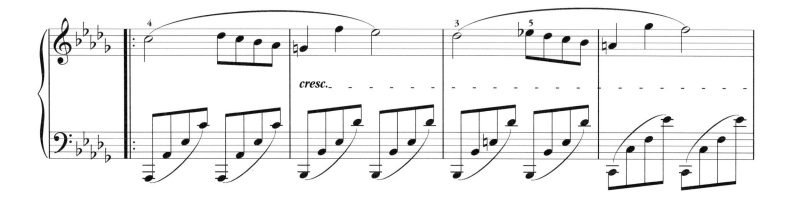

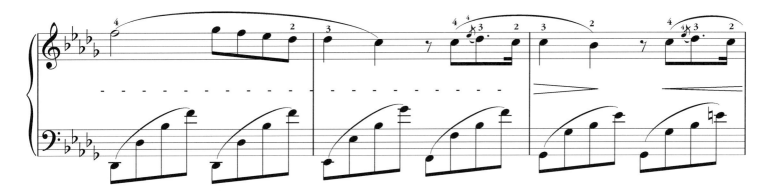

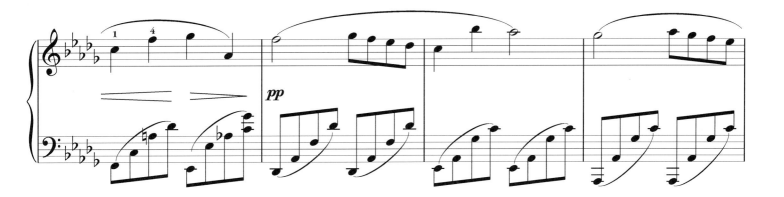

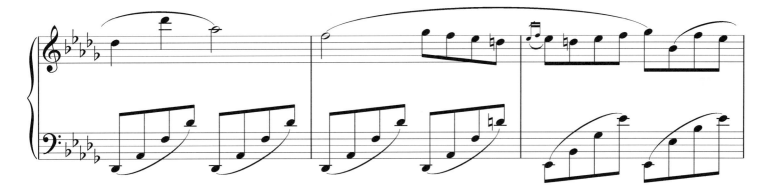

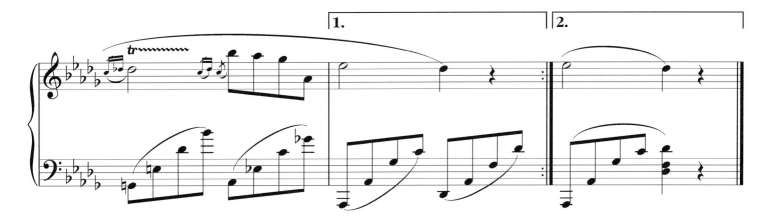

Prelude Op. 28, No. 15

'Raindrop'

Sostenuto

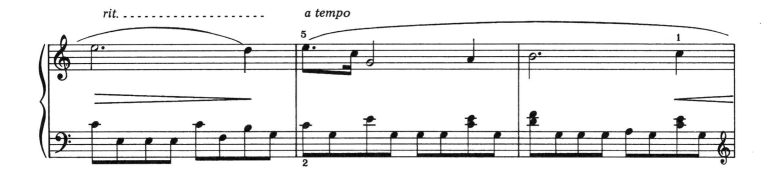

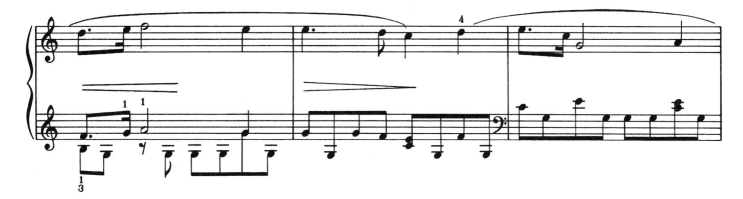

Waltz Op. 64, No. 2

Moderato

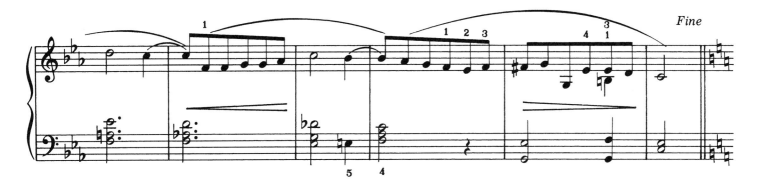

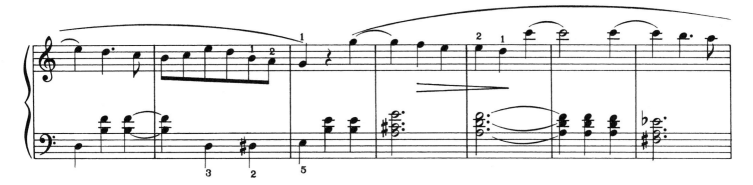

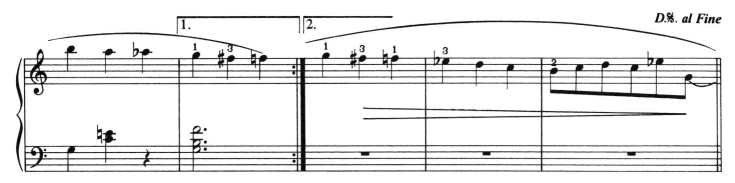

Etude No. 3

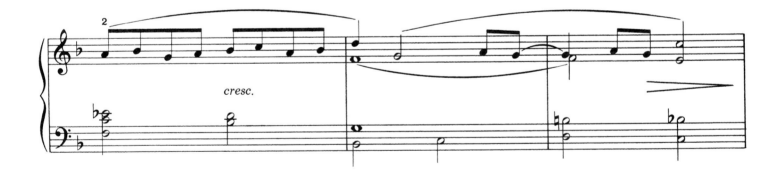

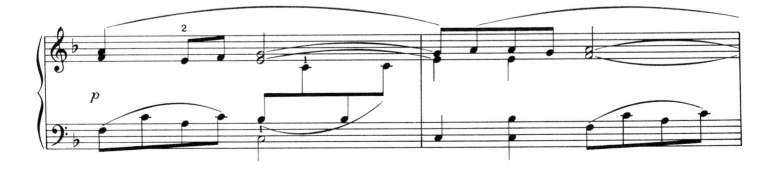

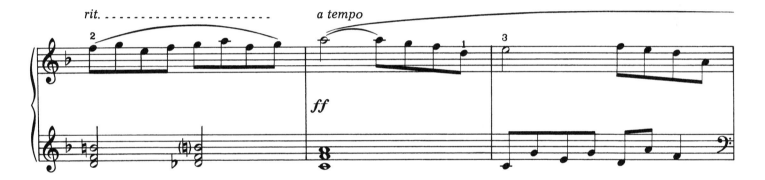

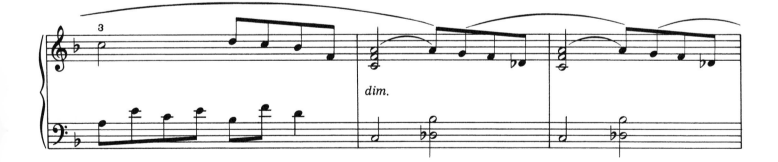

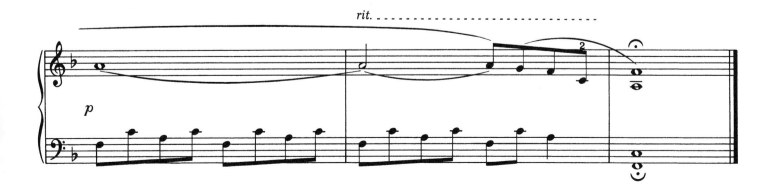

Ballade Op. 38

(Theme)

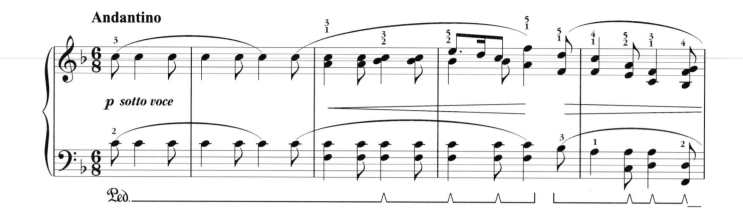

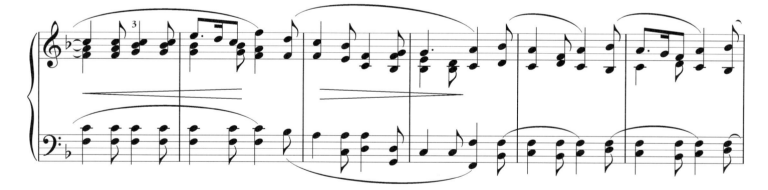

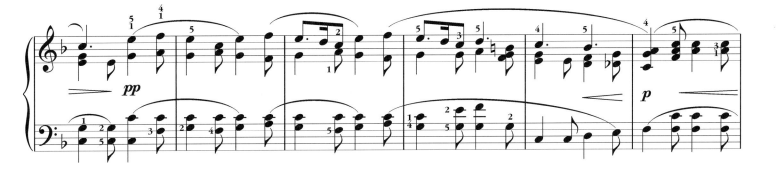

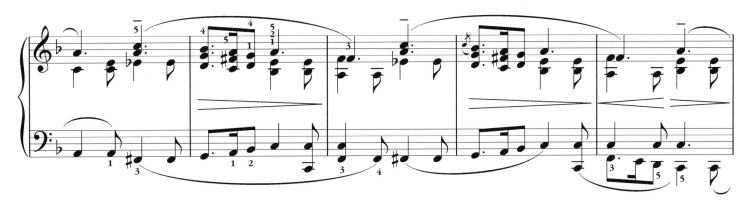

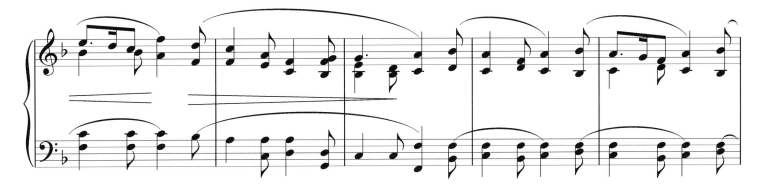

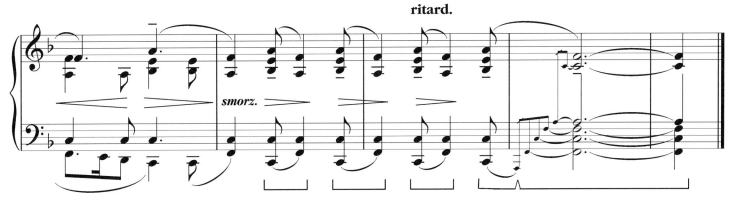

Chorale from Nocturne Op. 37, No. 1

Andante Sostenuto

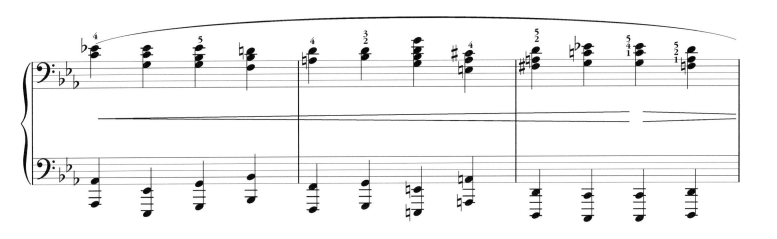

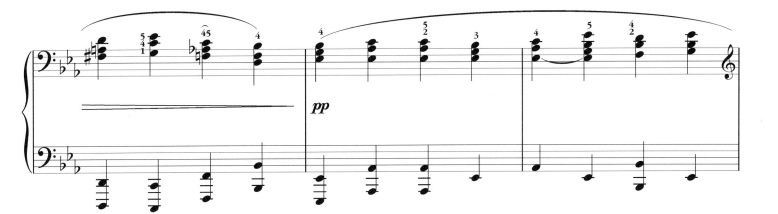

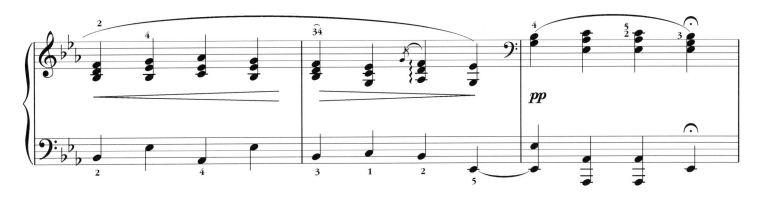

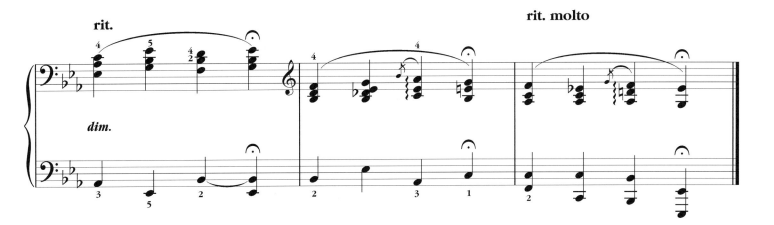

Prelude Op. 28, No. 20

Largo

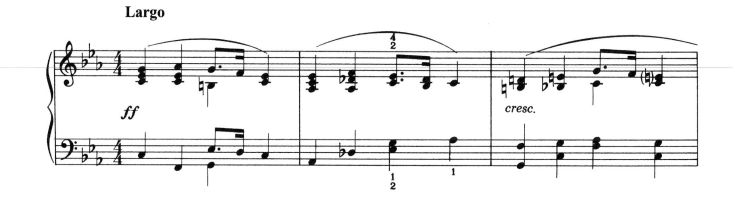

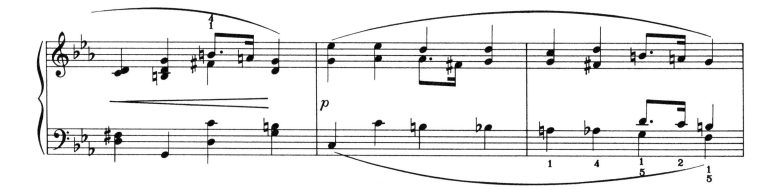

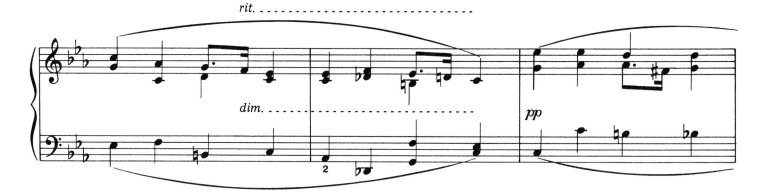

Mazurka Op. 67, No. 2

Cantabile

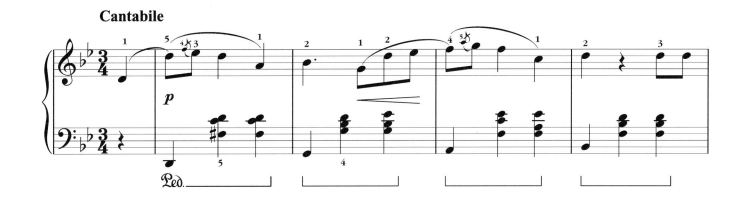

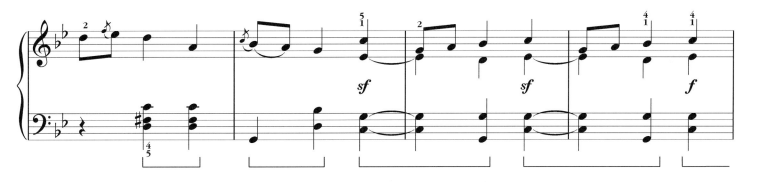

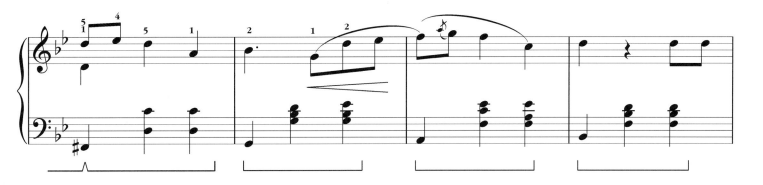

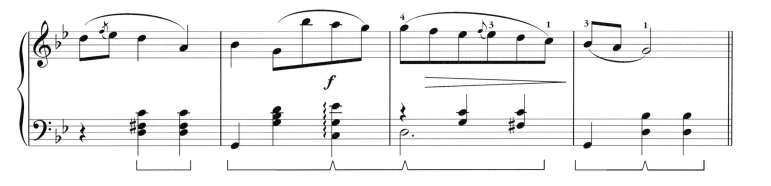

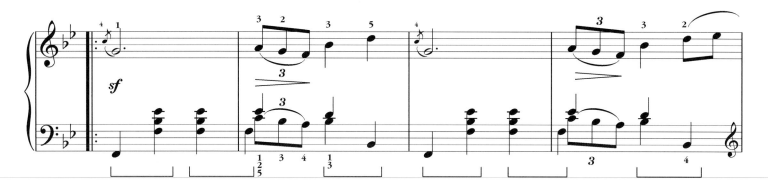

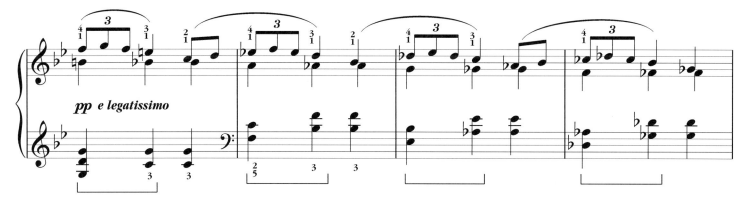

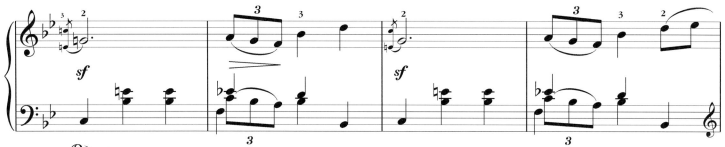

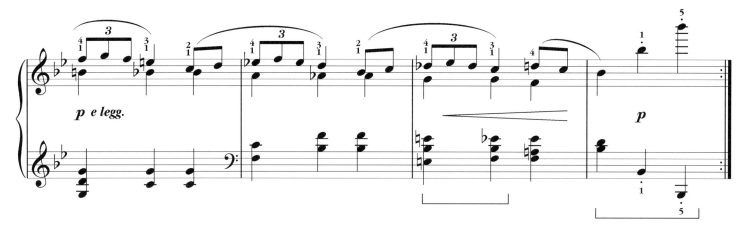

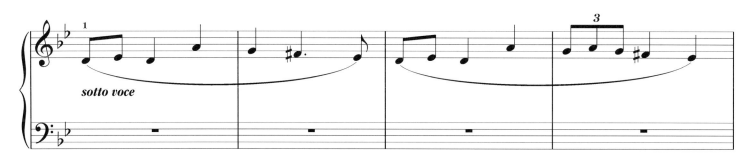

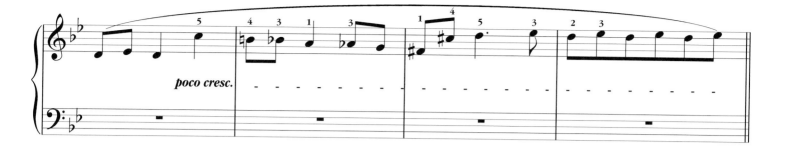

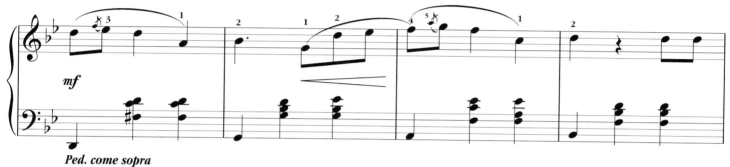

poco cresc.

mf

Ped. come sopra

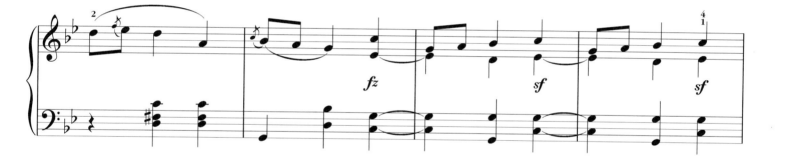

fz   sf   sf

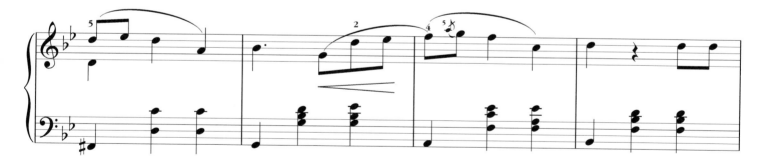

f

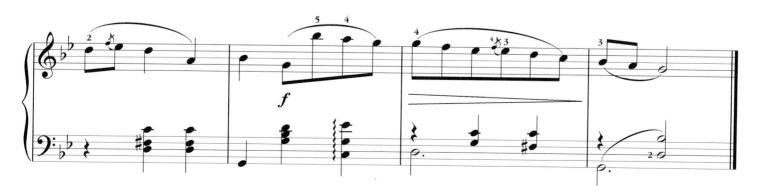

f